SHAH

NEMAT-UL-LAH

WALI

(RA)

PREDICTIONS

Translated by

Sayid Ashraf Shah

Become Shakespeare .com

ISLAMIC PRODUCTIONS SRINAGAR

First published in 2020 by

Becomeshakespeare.com
One Point Six Technologies Pvt Ltd.
1119-123, 1st Floor, Building J2, B - Wing,
Wadala Truck Terminal, Wadala East,
Mumbai, Maharashtra, India, 400022.
T:+91 8587995915

This book has been funded by WORDIT ART FUND
WORDIT ART FUND helps deserving
Authors publish their work
To apply for funding, please visit us at
becomeshakespeare.com

ISBN - 978-93-90266-80-7

DEDICATION

To Fehmida, Tawhida, Gowhar, Abida and Irfan.

In the name of Allah the Most Gracious the Most Merciful

PREFACE

The correction to the work of Shah Nematullah Sahib Wali has been conducted after scanning some ancient handwritten manuscripts, which are lying scattered with some ancient scholarly families. Efforts have been made that the right and correct verses are recorded.
Worthy readers are requested to point out and inform if they find any errors that persist, so that these can be rectified in future editions.

Seeker of prayers

Sayid Ashraf Shah

CONTENTS

About the work.	6
Translator's note	10
Qasida I.	11
Qasida II.	26
Qasida III.	33

About The Work

Hazrat Sayid Nematullah Shah Kimani (RA) was a great mystic and Wali saint of the eighth and ninth century Hijri. He was born in 734 H/1331 C and passed away in about 834 H/1431 C and lived for a hundred years of age. His birth place is Halab (Syria) but he spent his life at Samarqand, Herat, Yezd and Kirman (Mahan). His Sufi order of "Nemat-ul-lahi" is still sufficiently current in Iran and Faras.

Hazrat Shah Nematullah arrived in Mahan (Kirman) in 775H and started the order of guidance and righteousness. He has authored more than hundred books in Arabic and Persian besides pamphlets. Dr. Hamid professor of the University of Isfahan has conducted a lot of research on Shah Sahib.

According to Shah Sahib the Tasawuf is a special way of Tariqat and a collection of special religious beliefs and thoughts. Such beliefs have got manifest in Iran from very ancient times and these have expanded gradually. Next these beliefs got expressed with great force in the verses of poetry and prose. During Islamic period the beliefs of Irfan, Salook, and Sufism were presented through literature.

In Iran Tasawuf has two branches; one being negative which covers abandonment of the world and prayings, relations, killing desire of lust, adoption of contentment, poverty and lead a life of austerity. They deny all the attributes of the external world. Obviously this way has a lot of resemblance with Indian Sufism. The second branch of Irani Tasawuf is positive one and it pertains to the struggle in the path, desire, covering stages, sincerity, prayers, selflessness, service without any expectation, study, training the self, love, learning mystic knowledge (Marifat), reach the station of love of Allah and vanish in His Being and be steadfast on the direction of truth, trying without expecting any returns and doing selfless service.

This way the foundation of this Tasawuf has been laid on the serving, love and the understanding of Monotheism. The perfect Sufi is the one who acquires from others the knowledge of the stages of conformation and mediation and obtains the principles of speech and the arguments of logic and finds the path of the method of revelation, remembrance and the reality of the study of one's self and reaches the station of revelation and omnipresence of Allah. Make one's heart the place of manifestation of gallant love and affection and Monotheism, make one's thought reach the station studded with connection and with abundance of common inferiority, make one reach the station of the celestial world of oneness; keep clean the mirror of the conscience; can see manifestation of Allah within oneself; and be acquainted with the knowledge of Allah-(Marifat); become a manifestation of truth and reality in one's advices, sayings and speed. With this reflection of the shining vision observe the real unity among the world of human beings and understand that all the divisions and the religious quarrels are born because of the ignorance of man.

جون ندید ندحقیقت ره فسانه زدند

Shah Nematullah has described the mystical and Sufi beliefs in the best and sweetest verses. He has moulded the light and highly delicate feelings into diction. He has presented his mystic and Sufi beliefs in most graceful verse and literature:

منزل جان جهان بردر جانانه ماست
مسکن اهل دلان کوشهء میخانهء ماست
خلوتی بر در می خانه کرفتیم ولی
حرم قدس یکی کوشهء کاشانهء ماست
تا ز شمع رخ او مجلس جانان روشن شد
ا ز شمع رخ او مجلس جانان روشن شد د
دیده ای لولو ، لا لا که ز دریا آرند د
حاصل اشك جکر کوشهء جانانه ماست ت
تاابدکنج غمش درد دل ما خواهد بو د د
ز آنکه کنجش ز ازل درد دل ویرانهء ماست ت
ساقیانه ساغر و بیمانه سوی من آر آر
که مراد دو جهان یك لب بیمانه ماست ت

The predictions of Shah Nematullah Qadri (RA) have great importance in the Persian literature and have remained on the roof top of common fame and most of these have proved right till date. Shah Nematullah Qadri has expressed appropriately in the form of the Persian verse and it becomes known that he has got evidenced through revelation and inspiration and has not taken any help from any hints, allusion or hidden indications of future happenings or personalities, instead he has described these in such clear words that there remains possibility of not an iota of doubt and not only his stated names but also their titles by letters even have proved to be right, so much so he says:

بارینه قصه شویم در تازه قصه کویم ---- افتاد قرن دویم افتاد از زمانه
در ملك هند و بنکال اولاد کورکانی ---- شاهی کنند اما شاهی جو رستمانه
صاحب قران ثانی نیز آن کورکانی ---- شاهی کند اما شاهی جو حاکمانه

The Taimori dynasty is also called as Gorgani dynasty as well; so much so the seven generations of Amir Taimor ruled Hindustan for three hundred years, even Iran too was under their rule. The last king of this dynasty in India was Bahadur Shah Zafar. So while predicting the govermants of this dynasty at a separate place, he has quoted the names of all the kings and mentioned the future wars with other kings stating even about their conquest or defeat, while going through which it is felt that we are not reading the predictions but instead reading the history.

After the mention of all these kings he has described about the different types of the future events and happenings, which have come true perfectly. He has predicted the future independance of Hindustan and expressed his fear of the division of Hindustan as:

تقسیم هند گردد در دو حصص بیدا ---- آشوب و رنج بیدا از مکر و از بهانه

Next he has predicted the future painful events that shall occur after the division of the country. He has mentioned about the communal tension and the frightening scenes of massacre and has also advised Muslims to live with patience and respite and then he conveys a good news as well:

در عین بیقراری هنگام اضطراری ---- رحمی کند جون باری بر حال مومنانه

After stating all these events and happenings Hazrat Shah Nematullah (RA) becomes silent:

خاموش باش نعمت اسرار حق مکن فاش ---- در سال کنت کنزاً باشد جین بیانه

It is a fact that Shah Nematullah Qadri (RA) has been a perfect (Wali) saint, whatever prediction and revelation he has made, it can be the job of only a mystic and a perfect Wali only.

In fact the Sufi beliefs had got ingrossed in his etiquette, speech and character. He was of pleasing tongue, sweet speech, broken-hearted and kind. He would always feed the dervishes and never allowed space for malice in his heart. He was friend of all and would treat his enemies also with kindness and favour.

In his predictions there is reflected the influence, sweetness and mystic colour. Everyone finds something pleasant in these verses. May Allah bless him. Aameen!

TRANSLATOR'S NOTE

During the present turmoil of August-September, 2019 in Kashmir Valley almost whole business, transport, education, internt and other activities came to standstill and everyone was apprehensive about what was going to happen in future. Many talked about the Predictions of Hazrat Shah Nematullah Qadri born in 734 AH/1331 AD in Halab Syria and died in 834 AH/1431 AD at an age of 100 years. His predictions have come true word for word till date i.e. up to about 800 years after his death. Hence people are curious to read his predictions to prepare themselves for the events to come. The book was written in Persian and has already been translated into Urdu. There was a strong demand for an English version as most of the newly educated students are relatively unfamiliar with Persian and Urdu having studied in English medium schools. Hence I translated it into English language. I welcome suggestions for improvement.

Sayid Ashraf Shah.

October, 2019 AD/Safar, 1441 AH

QASIDA I.

Bismillah-ir-Rahman-ir-Rahim

In the name of Allah the Most Gracious the Most Merciful

Ignoring the ancient history I narrate the coming calamities of Hindustan, which will befall in miserable times.

The Gorgani tribe will rule with bravery on India and Bengal i.e. The tribe of Taimoris.

He will be the second "Sahib-i-Qiran" belonging to the progeny of Gorgan. He will rule in a way as it should be.

(Explanation: "Sahib-i-Qiran" is called the person at whose birth time both the sun and the moon are at 19 degrees of Zodiac sign Aries and this happens rarely. Both Amir Taimor and Alexander the great had the similar situation at their birth . Hence Alexandar the great was the first "Sahib-i-

Qiran" and Amir Taimor Gorgani the second "Sahib-i-Qiran". According to the astronomers the child who is born at such an hour is considered very lucky.)

For three hundred years his progeny shall rule the Hind and Bengal. They will conquer Kashmir and Nepal completely.

Their seven generations will rule Hindustan and Iran for seven generations, whereafter they will vanish in some corner.

(Explanation: In 1857 the Taimori kingdom ended, the last sign of which was Bahadur Shah Zafar,)

Luxury and gaiety will influence their hearts and the ways of bravery shall vanish suddenly.

The period that will follow, in this you will see the rise of Muslims will stop.

The people who will come as guests, will turn to be severe enemies also and will occupy the government. The enemies will run currency on their own name.

(Explanation: Purtagese, French, German and English people came to Hindustan and desired to have their foothold here but English people succeeded and occupied Hindustan, which continued from 1857 AD to 1947 AD.)

English people will commit plunder everywhere besides excesses and will snatch their government by cunningness and deciet.

(Explanation: Initially they constructed buildings for conducting trade. They obtained permission to install guns and cannons on these as a protection against the dacoits and converted these into forts slowly. Thus they gained access into the royal court and incited one Amir against the other creating disharmony between them till they paralysed the central government.)

The rulers will get intoxicated with wine and hemp and their country will be occupied forcefully by the English people.

The Christians shall be seen on the throne and they will snatch the government and power from Muslims by fraud and pretext.

They will resort to lot of killings and bloodshed. The people will die because of great hardship through their hands.

The Muslims will get frustrated from the war and these English people will be pursuing these Muslims like hunting hounds.

Suddenly there will be lot of publicity of this news among Muslims that a war has broken out between two infidel governments.

The two rulers of the governments will spell each other's ruin like a game of chess and will spend enough money to grab the country.

(Note: George V and Ceaser fought in Germany and lot of money was spent on armaments.)

After this there shall be a tough war for four years in Europe in which E (England) will find victory over G-(Germany) by fraud, deciet and trickery.

A major war will take place, whereby lot of massacre will occur and one crore thirty one lack souls will perish.

(Note: The first World War which started on 4th August 1914 AD and ended on 11th November 1918 AD at 11.11 AM. The British government appointed a commission to know the exact number of dead during the war, they prepared a report after one and a quarter year. In this the number of dead was stated to be one crore and over thirty lacks nearabout thirty one lacks.)

This war will last for six years, the 'E' will conquer 'G' by plundering.

(Note: By E is meant England and by G Germany)

After this there will occur war between Russia and Japan, wherein Japan will be the winner.

After the war ends, Russia and Japan will fix their separate borders but the treaty between them will be based on hypocrisy.

(Note: The result of this treaty manifested in the shape of World War, which started in 1939 AD. In 1904 Japan, in order to capture the area of Korea, had after declaring war against Russia arrested the Russian fleet of the Russian port Arthra and Velade Vastik in the river Azar and in 1905 arrested the remaining part of the sea fleet of Russia. Hence Russia had to forcibly enter into a treaty in 1908 after separating its borders with Japan.)

This treaty will be a weak one and not a permanent but temporary and deceitful.

The countries of Egypt, Sudan, Bukhara, Kohistan, Khatlan and the city of Karkhi and Tashkent will be taken.

(Note: Sudan fell in the hands of British and now it is free. Khatlan, Bukhara, Kohistan, Karkhi and Tashkent were occupied by Russia. Now these are free)

The Russians will occupy the port of Koh-i-Kaaf and will take the area from Khwarzm to Khiwa.

Next they will occupy fast Khizr and Gilaan and will fearlessly try to attack China and Iran as well.

From east to west you will see the infidels in power and this fact will be known to all.

The Islam and the Muslims will be rendered to poverty in Rum, Iran and Hindustan and Sindh almost all areas.

Two names by the names of Ahmad will mislead people; they will interpret Quran according to their own wishes.

One person will be from the progeny of Turks and will behave like the dacoit of devil and will tell a lie in the country of Hindustan and will slander.

Babonic plague and famine will spread in Hindustan; people will die everywhere. Muslims will die due to this cause.

(Note: This event too has occured in 1918 AD)

There will occur a calamitous ravishing earthquake in Japan, whereby one sixth in other way one sixteenth of

the country will perish.

(The calamitous earthquake that occured in the two cities of Japan Tokyo and Kopama in 1823 AD is well known)

This war of epidemic will continue for six years and will be the cause of death of people everywhere.

There will occur a ravishing earthquake in Hindustan, which will take place between Hind and Sindh.

(Note: In 1936 AD there occured an extremely severe earthquake in whole of Hindustan particularly in Quita and Bihar.)

G (Germany) and E (England) will remain silent but behind the screens they will prepare the equipment for war.

(Note: This equipment of war was used in the World War which started from 1939 AD)

When there will be war of Japan with China , the Christians too will come to fight alongwith them.

(Note: In 1933 AD there was war between Japan and China, it is a hint of the same)

After twenty one years of the first World War there will occur second World War, which will prove to be more disastrous than the first war due to its aggressive nature.

(Note: This was the second world war that started on 3rd September 1939 AD and ended on 9th May 1945 AD.)

In this war the equipmet to be used will be having flash like lightning and the ravishing calamitous armour.

(Note: The scientists of this period will invent instruments that will measure lightenings and ravishing armour like: rockets, Atom Bomb, Hydrojen Bomb etc.)

Yes if any one who is living in the east, he can hear the voice of the westerners and this voice shall be such as if it comes from the throne in the sky.

(Note: This verse points towards Radio and Telephone.)

First the French nation will be furious, next a war agreement will be signed between English and Italians.

The English and Greek army will fall down dead and a flood of water will emanate from absentia, which will be caused by due planning.

(Note: In the World War Germans at Padas at a mountain height of 2400 ft. (located in Greece) defeated Greeks, French and English armies, whereafter their feet could not stand on the land and many army soldiers fell in the ditches of the mountain and died there. (metaphor: died by ditch). Suddenly Germany attacked France breaking the dam on the river Reine, in the flood of which thousands of army men got drowned. This was solely the contrivance of the mind of General Rohail (metaphor : from the flood in absentia)-the concealed flood by one man's planning.)

Then one "A" hinting America second "E" hinting England besides Russia and Germany will become sweet like the mixture of milk and honey. Next one "I" and "G" will perish first and next the second "G" as well.

(Note: One I is meant to be Italy and G is meant to be Germany which will perish first)

They will swing swords like lightening and shower wrath like mountains till they will win the war by tricks and excuses.

This war will be fought for some years in sea and dry land and flood like fire will continue in all directions and fire armaments will also be used.

A calamitous earthquake will occur whereby one sixth of Japan will perish.

(Note: The secrets of German atom bomb fell in the hands of America and it dropped atom bomb on Japan, whereby Japan got destroyed -hint to Hiroshima)

English will leave India but they will sow the seeds of their evil deeds and wickedness for ever.

(Note: The English left India in 1947 but left Indians making them enemies of each other.)

A standard bearer will appear among the people wearing sacred thread, he shall be of lean and thin body and will talk like a brave man.

(Note: Karam Chandhar Gandhi was quite lean and thin and belonged to Hindu nation wearing sacred thread.)

The name of the petty businessman to take revenge of English people will start with letter "G". His name will have six letters. On seeing his kindness Muslims will become his friends or that this businessman will

become Muslim in his heart by the grace of God.

(Note: The real name of Gandhiji is Karam Chand. Gandhi is his alias. About his real name less people know. "G" hints towards "Ganghiji")
G A N D H I—6 letters, 6-ك ر م ج ن د letters

Hindustan will be divided into two parts. There will be mutual distress created by cunningness and fraud.

(Note: In 1947 AD Hindustan was divided; one part is named Hindustan and the other part Pakistan. By plunder and murder and devastation and mutual hatred every person will be displeased mutually.)

Rulers without crowns will rule and stupid and absurd orders will be issued, which will be all silly.

From the heart of Punjab (Lahore) Hindus will migrate and Muslims will occupy their property forcibly.

(Note: This event too occured in 1947. The Hindu population of Lahore migrated to Hindustan.)

Against this event in the city of Muslims (Delhi) the event will occur and Hindus will be forcible occupants.

The property and life of Muslims will be equally turned cheap and their blood will flow like rivers.

(Note: After the the division of Hindustan in 1947 the awkward event that occured on exchange of population; perhaps this hints at that.)

The government orders will remain hanging and neglected due to the bribery, laziness and negligence

and all this will be done knowingly.

The scholars will weep on their knowledge and so will do intellectuals on their intellect and unworthy people will be busy in enjoyment and nude dances.

The Muslim ummat of Prophet Muhammad (SAW) will commit limitless crimes and sinful acts.

The love and affection will get converted into carelessness and the respect and honour of elders will transform into bad etiquette and rudeness.

The chastity and sanctity will vanish totally and incidents of forced rape and kidnapping will occur.

Women will give up veil and males will get used to covering with veils. From outside women will look innocent but behind the curtain they shall prove to be unchaste.

Vulgar natured men, who will appear to be ascetic outwardly will be working as pimps for their daughters and others.

Sister with brother, boys with their mothers, fathers with their daughters will commit acts of crime and will be crimnals in love and passion.

The desire for salat prayers, fasting, zakat-alms giving, Hajj pilgrimage and charity will end, instead, these will become undesirable.

The sinners will have upper hand on the people and the respect of the good people will vanish.

The infidels will stop the faithful from performing religious rights and obstruct performing Hajj pilgrimage and acquire Quranic education.

(And once the English Viceroy has acted accordingly and it is happening now-a-days too.)

The people will fearlessly drink wine in the cities, forests, and in mountains. They will inhale hashish and its alternative. The intoxication will become a common affair in hotels, parties and at the time of the picnics in gardens.

The directions of Islam will extinguish like the lamps. The people will consider the scholars as ignorant men and the ignorant people as the scholars.

The wickedness and immorality will spread in all directions, so much so mother will make excuses from her daughter and vice versa.

In Madrasas and Maktabas people will learn the knowledge of astrology and will become ignorant of Fiqh and Tafsir.

The scholars will depict their eminence by decorating their crests of turbans, but there will be the idols of Samiri hidden in their clothes.

(Note: It means that outwardly the scholars will look to be all praying but inside, they will be full of mischief and will be misled.)

And these scholars will be greatly misled, who will mislead the nation by wearing turbans inspite of their incapability.

The Scholars and Muftis will issue futwas against the religion and will violate the directions of Shariat openly.

With the feeling of great suffering , I say with great anxiety to abandon this way of Christianity (ways of Christians).

A great calamity will occur which will be suitable for this type of evil deeds and Allah will Himself issue an order of murder.

Muslims will get killed and destroyed. All this will happen through the hands of spearmen lancer Hindu people.

(Note: This can mean Rashtrya Sevak Sangh who are laced with spears)

The own leaders of Muslims will be friends of Hindus behind the curtain, they will plan and help them according to their sinful promise

The people of Hindustan will help them but will remain unaware that after proceding ahead, their this assistance will go waste.

This event will occur between two Eids when the moon will pass between the two destinations and the sun will pass the fiftieth axial diameter of the twelveth bastion sign of zodiac and the Hindus will be considered disgraced in the sight of whole world, i.e. Shahnoor meaning the sun will be in the stage of Cancer and the cruel will be condemned the world over.

(Note: According to Pandit Manohar Ram's predictions this

revolution of stars has occured last year against Pakistan. Besides this the other researches are not nearer to this analogy.)

An auspicious month will become the biggest occasion of execution and in every house there will be martyrs like those of Kerbala.

(Note: The auspicious month i.e. The month of Ramadhan; this month is called a special month in Arabic, when people's eyes are fixed on the moon when they wait to sight the Eid moon. "*Ghyas-ul-lughat*". It should be clear that in this auspicious month there was mass murder in former East Pakistan and in every house everywhere there was a martyrdom like Karbala.)

In quite restlessness Allah will bless Muslims with mercy.

Suddenly Muslims will get a good news and there will start a vallant war with infidels.

In the coming Muharram the sword will come in the hands of Muslims and they will launch offensive aggression.

Besides a friend of God (Habibullah) who will have the status of "Sahibiqiran" will pull out sword from the sheath with the help of Allah.

The earth will start shaking by the march of brave Muslim soldiers of the borders, who will penetrate forcefully with the aim of success.

They will attack overnight like ants and locust swarm till Afghan nation will achieve success.

(Note: By ants is meant the land army and locust swarm can mean air force.)

From the forests, mountains and deserts and rivers, the rough Arabs will gush forth like a flood at fast speed from all directions laced with fire arms.

The Afghans, Iranis and Deccanis (i.e. Baluch) will join together; these people will conquer whole of Hindustan with valour.

They will conquer the cities of Punjab, Delhi, Kashmir, Deccan and Jammu with unknown assistance from Allah.

All the malicious of the religion and faith will be killed and whole of India will be cleared of the Hindu customs.

Like Hindustan the destiny of Europe too will turn bad and the third world war will begin.

Among the two E's that I have mentioned, one E (England) will join the war like an unbridled horse and Russia will attack the second E (western Europe)

(Note: One Alif means America and second Alif means انكليندEngland; R means Russia)

The defeated G (Germany) will join with Russia and come alongwith volcanic armaments of hell.

E (England) English people will vanish in such a manner that their name will not exist except in the pages of history.

This punishment will be met from the unknown, it will be attributed to the sinner and the Christian civilisation can not raise its head again.

This war will continue fiercely for a few years both in sea and land in saline and salt waters.

The unfaithful will destroy whole world, at last they will become the fuel for hell.

(Note: Due to above cited verse Lord Curzon had banned this Qasida. It is also reported that on hearing the news of war on 6th August 1914 AD Abu Bakr Shah the son of Bahadur Shah Zafar had recited these verses extempore:)
"The messenger from Europe has brought the message of war; thanks to Allah the blood of martyrs has brought its result."
Thereafter this Qasida was banned more strictly.

The secret that I have related openly and strung like pearls, will serve you as a help and for success as a teacher from the unknown.

If you want victory and that too quickly then for God's sake follow the commandments of God.

Suddenly in the period of Hajj Hazrat Mahdi will emerge, who will become famous the world over.

When the auspicious initial period of the year "KANA ZAHOOQA" will begin, then Imam Mahdi with the certificate of Mahdism will emerge gracefully.

O' Nemat be silent, don't reveal the secrets of God, when the year according to Ayat "KUNTU KANZAN" will come, that day all that will occur.

QASIDA II.

(01)

I am telling the truth that a king will be born in the world whose name will be Taimor Shah Sahibqiran.

(02)

After him there will appear a conqueror Chief king who will be the successor of Taimor Shah Sahibqiran's kingdom.

(03)

When he will leave from the temporal world to the lasting world, after these events, a king will appear whose rule shall be evident to one and all.

(04)

After this the master of necks "King of kings Umar" the claimant of kingdom will be born. From him kindness will get manifest.

(05)

After this the king of Kabul Babar will become the king of Hindustan.

(06)

When the time of rule of Sikandar Shah Lodhi to Ibrahim Shah Lodhi will reach, be sure there will spread mischief and disturbance in this country.

(07)

Then will come the turn of Himayun and from the unknown, from Allah an Afghan will revolt.

(08)

King Himayun will meet an accident (that is) A king named Sher Shah Suri will be born (as a claimant of the kingdom).

(09)

King Himayun will go to the prince of the king of Iran the son of king Rasool so that with the help of this worthy king, his honour, status and authority is

restored.

(10)

The king of Iran will make many favours to him, this will get manifest by restoration of his honour, status like other kings.

(11)

So much so he will attack Hindustan with his army, Sher Shah will die and his son will be born to be (the successor of the kingdom).

(12)

After this king Himayun will occupy Hindustan; next the King of kings Jalal-ud-din Mohammad Akbar will become the king.

(13)

After this the king of kings the protector of the world Jahangir will be born. When he arrives as if the moon will rise on the fourteenth night.

(14)

When king Jahangir leaves on his last journey, after him "Shah Jahan Sahib-i-qiran second"will become the king.

(15)

Shah Jahan will rule for more than one Qaran-(38 years) and less than forty years and during this period a son will be born to him.

(16)

The country will get destroyed and disturbance will spread in the world. If water and bread becomes available in this period, it must be considered as one of the wonders.

(17)

When such will be the condition of the world-(Jahan), the people will be absorbed in wonder. The star Jupiter will appear splashing fire from the sky.

(18)

The truth will lessen, falsehood, trickery, deception will increase. Friends will turn to be enemies and there will spread rivalry and jealousy among them.

(19)

Thus Shah Jahan will continue to rule, his period of governance shall last for twenty years till one of his sons will become a distinguished one.

(20)

He will raise his voice in the world and he will be the king besides a guardian of the mistresses of the creation of the world.

(21)

Meanwhile a king will be born whose name will be

"Muazam"

(22)

In his period people will gather together and peace will be established as if he will serve as an ointment to the wounds of the world.

(23)

He will remain as a king for a few years likewise. After his death his son will become his successor.

(24)

By the blessing of his arrival the order of the world will get balanced; worry and jealousy will vanish and a period of happiness and enjoyment will prevail.

(25)

After this a powerful king Mohammad Shah will come to Hindustan and will rule there.

(26)

He will remain the ruler for twenty one years as such. When his rule will be over, a Chief will be born

(27)

When that sovereign will leave for the lasting world, there will take place a fissure in his dynasty.

(28)

Nadir Shah will come from Iran to snatch the throne of Hindustan; with the power of his sword there will be massacre in Delhi.

(29)

After this king Babar will rule for a few days. In his period a Faqir close to God will be born.

(30)

His name will be Nanak, world will bow to him, he will become very popular.

(31)

His fame will spread in the country of Punjab. The nation of Sikhs will be his disciple and he will be their preceptor.

(32)

The Sikh tribe will deal very cruelly with Muslims. This atrocity will continue in this country for forty years.

(33)

After this English people will conquer Hindustan and their rule will continue in Hindustan for a hundred years.

(34)

Since in the English period cruelty and tyranny will be the order of the day, (so) for their defence a king from the west will arise.

(35)

There will be many fierce wars between the English people and the western invader king. Undoubtedly a world will be murdered in this war.

(36)

The efforts of the western king will succeed and the Christians will be defeated utterly.

(37)

For forty years there will prevail mastery of Islam in Hindustan, after this Dajjal will emege from Isfahan.

(38)

Listen to me, for the annihilation of this Dajjal Eisa (AS)- (Jesus Christ) will arrive and Mahdi of last times will be born.

(39)

It was 570 AH or 580 AH when this prediction was made and in 1380 AH all these events will occur.

(40)

Nemat Shah has been informed of the unknown facts, his sayings will get manifest to people definitely.

QASIDA III.

YA FATTAH
(O' The Opener-of the door of success)

(1)

I am witnessing the power of God and observing the events of the time.

(2)

I am not stating on the basis of astrology but instead observing by the depiction of the Creator God.

(3)

There will spread mischief and disturbance in Egypt, Syria and Iraq.

(4)

This will not be the state of affairs of one country only , instead in this period all the countries will suffer due to disorder, war and conflict.

(5)

I hear a strange story, I can view tension and conflict between the countries.

(6)

I am seeing killing, murder of many armies on my right and left.

(7)

I see scholars and teachers are mean and ungenerous.

(8)

I see religious beliefs as weak and also observe people feeling proud of these weak beliefs.

(9)

I see the respectful people of all nations sad and disgraced.

(10)

I see workers being dismissed after being entrusted with posts and they face poverty and are annoyed and this will happen behind the curtain.

(11)

I see Turks and Tajiks pitted to fight against each other.

(12)

I see everywhere cunningness and cheating from young and old.

(13)

The garden of virtue is ruined and I see it to be the place of gathering of wicked and naughty people.

(14)

I see if there is peace anywhere today, it is in the boundaries of mountains.

(15)

Though I see all these scenes, still there is nothing to worry as along with this I see a joy to counter the sorrow.

(16)

This year and after some years I see the world decorated like a beloved.

(17)

I see a clever and prudent king as a dignified ruler.

(18)

The sayings relate differently; it seems as if I don't see all this when I am awake.

(19)

After passing of 1200 years, I see strange events taking place.

(20)

In the mirror of the conscience-striken world, I see the dust of mischiefs, the rust of the sins and the clouds of jealousy.

(21)

The atrocities of cruel people will touch great heights in the countries.

(22)

In between and on its borders many mischiefs and disturbances will arise and there will be war and cruelty.

(23)

Such a revolution will occur that master will become the slave and the slave the master.

(24)

Previous year those who carried burden of one person, this year I see his heart compressed under the burden.

(25)

The first kingdom will go and new currency will be issued, which will be of lesser value.

(26)

I see the kings of the world entangled with one another.

(27)

I see the face of moon as dark and the heart of sun wounded.

(28)

I see the tradesmen of far off countries lying on the routes tired.

(29)

I see the condition of Hindus very bad and the atrocities of Turk dynasties.

(30)

I see famines spreading and gardens not bearing fruits.

(31)

I observe that now one must remain separate, be patient and go into seclusion.

(32)

But one should not worry in this period of anxiety and mischief as I observe that the joy of meeting of a friend

is hidden in between these disturbances.

(33)

When autumn season will be over, the sun of spring will rise.

(34)

When his perid will pass successfully, his son will remain as a heritage of his memory.

(35)

There will be all slaves and kings to serve him in his presence.

(36)

He will be the ruler of the whole world and the king of great dynasty.

(37)

His outer and inner self will resemble a prophet and knowledge and toleration will be his habit.

(38)

In his possession is the shining hand, then I see him along with the double edged sword.

(39)

By him the Shariat will be refreshed and the buds of religion will bear fruits.

(40)

O' my brother, the regime of this royal horse rider will last for forty years.

(41)

The opponents and disobedient of this Imam also passed away, for whom there is destined shame and repentance at last.

(42)

He is such a conqueror, who is a friend of friends and killer of the enemies. I find him true sympathiser and well-wisher of God's creation.

(43)

I see that by his arrival Shariat will get bedecked and Islam will flourish and the Mohammadan religion of strong rope will strengthen and be secured.

(44)

I see that the treasure of Ceasar and the wealth of Alexandar all are put to use.

(45)

I see that later on he will become Imam himself and the world will (depend) on him.

(46)

I read A, H, M, D and see this will be the name of this celebrity.

(47)

By his arrival the religion will thrive and the world as well as people will become prosperous.

(48)

He will be Mahdi and Eisa (Jesus) of his time. I see both these facts in this horse rider.

(49)

I see this world bedecked like Egypt and the justice of this Imam will serve as shelter for the people.

(50)

This king of mine will have seven wazirs and all of them will be successful.

(51)

I see pleasing wine in the hands of the cup-bearer of the Monotheism.

(52)

I see the swords of stone hearted persons rusted and undependable.

(53)

I see in the pasture along with sheep and goats, lions

and dears moving together with great complacency.

(54)

I see Abbar Turks as lazy and their enemy intoxicated.

(55)

I see Nematullah sitting aloof all alone in a corner.

BOOKS PUBLISHED BY ISLAMIC PRODUCTIONS SRINAGAR

1. معجزه محمدی کا لافانی تسلسل
2. بسم الله کی تفسیر
3. فضیلت کی راتین
4. حرمت کی مهینی
5. کشمیرکنی جند بزرك عالم و صوفی
6. جنوبی هند مین اسلام کی ابتداء
7. بابا بام الدین
8. معجزه قرآن
9. مومن کامل کی اوصاف
10. هماری اسلاف اور مشائخ کشمیر
11. مرغوب القلوب
12. خواجه حبیب الله عطار
13. تزکره سالکین کشمیر
14. Let the World know.
15. The Truth
16. Srinagar-the Sun City
17. Fragrant Flowers
18. The Pearls of Deep Sea
19. Glimpses of Paradise
20. Our Concern
21. My Life Story
22. My Reflections
23. My Recollections
24. My Musings
25. Our New Concerns
26. Awrad-i-Fathiah
27. Kibryat-i-Ahmer
28. Dalail-ul-Khairat
29. Qasida Burdah
30. Hizb-ul-Bahar
31. The Unchallenged Truth
32. Kareema Maulood-i-Barzanji

33. Saints of Kashmir.
34. Environment in Jammu & Kashmir.
35. Sufi Saints of Kashmir. (Partridge Publishing.com/India)
36. Sufi Saints of Kashmir, Sufi Orders of Kashmir. (Gulshan Books Residency Road Srinagar.)
37. Kashmir-Jhelum Valley Civilization.
38. Hazrat Mir Mohammad Sayid Hussain Simnani (RA)
39. Shajra Sadat- (Tarikh-i-Kashmir)
40. Islam in Kashmir.
41. Maqamat-i-Eishan
42. The Wonderful Miracles of Kashmiri Sufi Saints
43. Biography of Shah-i-Hamadan (RA)
44. Sayings of Shaikh-ul-Alam (RA)-(under process.)
45. Tarikh-i-Azmi -(under process-UP)
46. Minhaj-ul Arifin (Hazrat Amir-i-Kabir RA)
47. Rubayat-i-Hazrat Khwaja Naqshband (RA)
48. Treatise of Hazrat Khwaja Ansari (RA)
49. Predictions of Shah Nematullah Qadri (RA)
50. Shajra Tariqat Suhrawardy Order in Kashmir.
51. My Paternal family tree from Hazrat Adam (AS)
52. My Maternal family tree from Hazrat Umar (RA).

ABOUT THE TRANSLATOR

Er. Mohammad Ashraf Fazili who writes under the pen name Sayid Ashraf Shah received his early education from The University of Kashmir, Srinagar and a degree in engineering from Annamalai University, Tamil Nadu with Honors in 1963. He served in PWD, J&K for forty years and retired as a Chief Engineer. Presently he is a chartered engineer, consultant, and Fellow Institution of Engineers India (FIE). Having served as chairman The Institution of Engineers (India) J&K State Centre, he is a member of various professional organizations like the Institution of Engineers (India) Kolkata, World Federation of Engineers Organization (IMWFEO), Indian Road Congress (MIRC) and American Society of Civil Engineers (MASCE). He has authored or compiled over 40 books and presented over eighty papers in national and international seminars. He continues to be a columnist and a freelance writer. He has traveled widely in India and abroad. He has personally contributed about three hundred manuscripts and rare books from his ancestral collection to the Allama Iqbal Library, The University of Kashmir, Srinagar.